WRITE ABOUT IT

Primary

by Imogene Forte

Incentive Publications, Inc.   Nashville, Tennessee

Thank You

to Mary Catherine Mahoney

and to Susan Oglander

editors

to Becky Cutler

cover designer

and to Mary Hamilton

artist

ISBN   0-86530-045-3

These Adventures in Writing Belong to

_____

TABLE OF CONTENTS

WRITE ABOUT IT . . .

Ideas for Young Writers

- Look for new words in every book you read.
- Learn to spell one new w   every day.
- Write to a pen pal.
- Keep a diary.
- Write a play.
- Make lists of words & phrases   at c
  excitement, describe and
  demand attention.
- Daydream, and write
  down your dreams.

WRITE ABOUT IT was written to provide interesting, fun-filled activities to help boys and girls achieve writing independence. Each page has been carefully designed to reinforce and extend one or more writing skills. Easy-to-follow directions, fanciful contemporary-based themes, and the use of a controlled but not limited vocabulary encourage purposeful personal writing.

To simplify classroom or home use, the reproducible activity pages have been organized into two broad areas:

I. Vocabulary development and technical writing skills
   A. Parts of speech
   B. Word usage
   C. Word meanings
   D. Punctuation and capitalization
   E. Writing sentences and paragraphs

II. Composition and original writing
   A. Organizing ideas
   B. Special literary devices
   C. Prose and poetry

Each of the worksheets is designed to stand alone and provide one complete writing experience. They may be used to supplement and reinforce adopted courses of study and are appropriate for use in individual or group settings. For classroom use, teachers will want to review the skills as listed in the table of contents and plan the order and manner of presentation to meet student needs. In a home or other setting where the book is used individually, the pages will fall into a natural skills sequence and can be used most efficiently in the order presented.

The purposes of this collection of read-think-and-write activities are to encourage kids to stretch their minds, develop their imaginations, and enjoy the thrill of successful writing.

Get your pencil; WRITE ABOUT IT!

Imogene Forte

VOCABULARY DEVELOPMENT
and
TECHNICAL WRITING SKILLS

A WRITER'S RECORD

Real writers say that the best way to become a great writer is to write, write, write.
Begin your writing record today.

_____ 's Writing Record
(your name)

Things To Write	Date
☐ Ad _____	_____
☐ Autobiography _____	_____
☐ Cartoon _____	_____
☐ Greeting card _____	_____
☐ Jokes _____	_____
☐ Letter _____	_____
☐ Lists _____	_____
☐ Note _____	_____
☐ Paragraph _____	_____
☐ Play _____	_____
☐ Poetry _____	_____
☐ Report _____	_____
☐ Sentences _____	_____
☐ Story _____	_____

Save your writing... you'll love reading it later!

NAME YOUR HOBBY

A *noun* is the name of a person, place, or thing.
Write the name of your favorite hobby.

_____

Write as many nouns as you can think of that are
related to that hobby.

14

A JUMPING RIDDLE

What animal comes from
   Australia,
      jumps all about,
         and has a full pouch?

Fill in the letters to find out.

_____
  1

_____ _____ _____ _____ _____ _____
 13   15   20   8   5   18

_____ _____ _____ _____ _____ _____ _____ _____
 11   1   14   7   1   18   15   15

_____ _____ _____ _____
 23   9   20   8

_____ _____ _____ _____ _____
 20   8   18   5   5

_____ _____ _____ _____ _____ _____
  2   1   2   9   5   19

A B C D E F G H
1 2 3 4 5 6 7 8

I J K L M N O
9 10 11 12 13 14 15

P Q R S T U
16 17 18 19 20 21

V W X Y Z
22 23 24 25 26

Write action words to tell 5 more things the animal can do.

_____

_____

_____

_____

_____

VERBS ON THE GO

Write 3 verbs that show some action that would be possible for each of the nouns pictured below. (Use your dictionary if you need spelling help.)

CREATE A CREATURE

Use your crayons to color this creature.
Write 5 words to describe your creature.
Use the words to write a story about it.

1. _____

2. _____

3. _____

4. _____

5. _____

_____

_____

_____

_____

_____

_____

_____

_____

_____

_____

_____

_____

_____

A DAY AT THE ZOO

Adjectives are used to help readers see a person, place, or thing as the writer sees it.

The writer of the paragraph below used too many adjectives.

Rewrite the paragraph using fewer adjectives to make the paragraph clearer and more interesting.

The zoo was a wonderful, noisy, exciting place. The funny monkeys, with their frisky but simple expressions, were always delightful. There were cages full of fancy, beautiful, delicate birds of every color and size. On one side were the wild animals — ferocious-looking lions; big, burly bears; and some of the tallest, giant giraffes imaginable. Of course, one of the best things about the zoo was the baby animals. The cute, soft baby ducks and the adorable, friendly lambs seemed so glad to see us. A day at the zoo was the nicest, most pleasant way to spend a sunny Sunday afternoon.

WHO IS MS. NAME TO-DO-LO?

An adjective is a word that describes or gives a fuller picture of a noun.

This creature is a Name To-Do-Lo. She lives on a cold mountaintop in a faraway land. Write an adjective on each of her spots to tell about her.

GET TO THE COTTAGE

To find your way through the forest and get safely back to the cottage, color in all the spaces that contain a word that can be used as both a noun and a verb.

MENU MAGIC

Mr. Mack will open his new cafe soon.

He plans to serve good, plain food, but he wants a fancy menu.

Look at the word list to find a more colorful word for each underlined word.

Write the new word on the line to make Mr. Mack's menu interesting.

Word list:

juicy	tasty
delicious	fancy
whipped	wonderful
super	hot

Mack's <u>Fine</u> _____ Cafe

<u>cooked</u> _____ beef

<u>fresh</u> _____ beans

<u>mashed</u> _____ potatoes

<u>plain</u> _____ spinach

<u>warm</u> _____ muffins

<u>great</u> _____ pie

<u>good</u> _____ layer cake

A PARROT'S LUCK

In this story about a parrot, you will find 7 underlined words.

Copy the story on the lines below, changing each underlined word by writing a word that has the opposite meaning.

Then finish the story.

A <u>Day</u> in the <u>Sunlight</u>

One <u>morning</u>, Polly Parrot realized that she was in the <u>city</u>. She wondered if she was having a dream. It was very <u>light</u> outside, and everything was <u>noisy</u>. Polly wanted to go out. She put on her <u>white</u> coat and headed for the door.

HOMONYM HIKERS

A *homonym* is a word that is pronounced the same as another word but is spelled differently and has a different meaning.

Fill in the blanks below with the correct homonym.

sun, son
eight, ate
sea, see

tale, tail
won, one
wait, weight

1. On the first day of their camping trip, Mr. Worthington and his _____ Tommy woke up early to watch the _____ rise.
2. They were hungry and, after cooking _____ eggs and some bacon, they _____ breakfast.
3. Then they felt ready to hike up a nearby mountain so they could _____ the _____ below.
4. They had heard a _____ about a sea monster that had a twenty-foot-long _____ .
5. They made a bet about whether the monster would appear, but by _____ o'clock Tommy gave up and said his dad had _____ the bet.
6. He said he didn't want to _____ any longer, and he said they would lose _____ if they didn't eat lunch soon!

SHOULD WE OR SHOULDN'T WE?

Some words can be used more than one way in a sentence.

Read the sentences below.

Select the word from the word list that best fits each blank.

You will use the words more than once.

Word list:

well   visit   cold

1. Is Grandma feeling _____ now?

2. Tomorrow we hope to_____ her.

3. She always looks forward to our _____ .

4. Last week she had a _____ , so we didn't see her.

5. The weather outside is still_____ , and it might be easy to get sick.

6. _____ , maybe we should see her the next day instead.

ABBREVIATED TOUCHDOWN

When Obal from the planet Grindal landed his spaceship on Earth, he sent back a report to the fleet commander. Read Obal's computer report, and circle all the abbreviations in it. Then write the abbreviations from his report and all the words they stand for on the computer printout below.

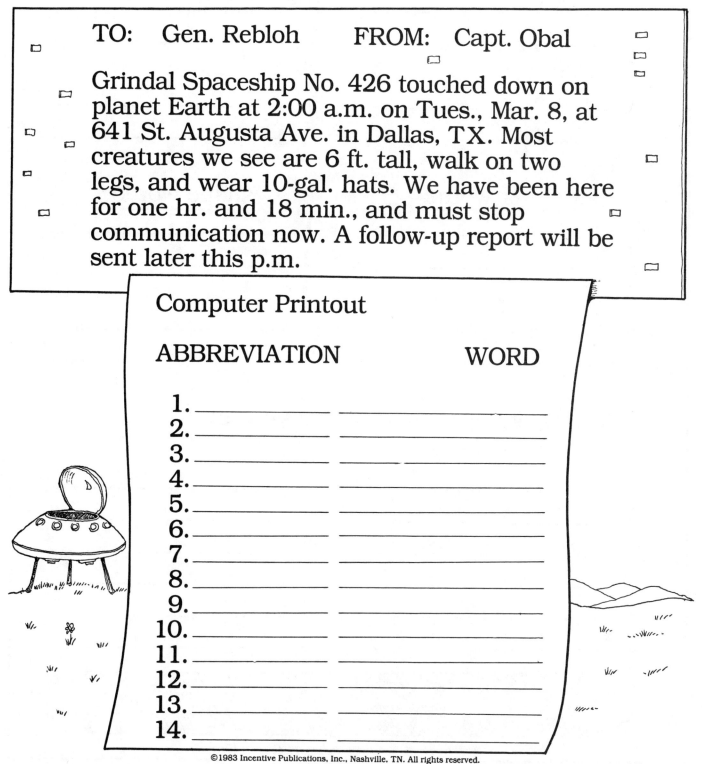

TO: Gen. Rebloh   FROM: Capt. Obal

Grindal Spaceship No. 426 touched down on planet Earth at 2:00 a.m. on Tues., Mar. 8, at 641 St. Augusta Ave. in Dallas, TX. Most creatures we see are 6 ft. tall, walk on two legs, and wear 10-gal. hats. We have been here for one hr. and 18 min., and must stop communication now. A follow-up report will be sent later this p.m.

Computer Printout

ABBREVIATION	WORD
1.	
2.	
3.	
4.	
5.	
6.	
7.	
8.	
9.	
10.	
11.	
12.	
13.	
14.	

LIST-MAKER'S LISTS

Write 5 words for each word list below.
The first one has been done for you.

<u>feeling words</u>

1. <u>sad</u>
2. <u>happy</u>
3. <u>lonely</u>
4. <u>friendly</u>
5. <u>angry</u>

<u>cold words</u>

1. _____
2. _____
3. _____
4. _____
5. _____

<u>weather words</u>

1. _____
2. _____
3. _____
4. _____
5. _____

<u>shape words</u>

1. _____
2. _____
3. _____
4. _____
5. _____

Now make up 2 word lists of your own.

_____

1. _____
2. _____
3. _____
4. _____
5. _____

_____

1. _____
2. _____
3. _____
4. _____
5. _____

CLICHES ON THE LINE

Some expressions are used so often that they become boring.

Each of the following sentences contains such an expression.

Write a sentence telling what you think each underlined phrase means.

1. I <u>heaved a sigh of relief</u> when the roller-coaster ride was over. _____
   _____

2. My pencil must have <u>vanished into thin air</u>.
   _____
   _____

3. Sometimes my brother <u>burns the midnight oil</u>.
   _____
   _____

4. <u>It dawned on me</u> that it was my mother's birthday. _____
   _____

5. <u>As the crow flies</u>, Ed's house is 5 minutes from my house. _____
   _____

6. I like <u>each and every one</u> of my brother's friends. _____
   _____

7. The haunted house left me <u>at a loss for words</u>. _____
   _____

HOT OR COLD

This igloo was built with "cold" words.
Warm it up by adding "hot" words.
Use some of the words to write a sentence telling
about the people who live in the igloo.

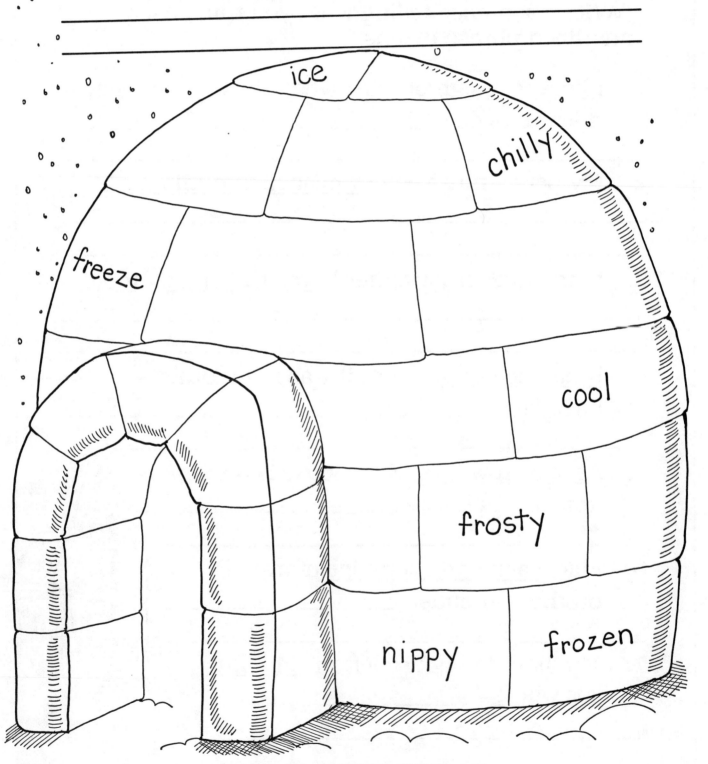

SAY IT ANOTHER WAY

Good writers are constantly looking for new and different words to use to make their writing more interesting.

Here are 5 other ways to say *hurry*.

1. rush
2. run
3. speed
4. race
5. hasten

Use your dictionary to find 5 or more words that could be used to replace each of the following words.

	hurt		old		little
1.	_____	1.	_____	1.	_____
2.	_____	2.	_____	2.	_____
3.	_____	3.	_____	3.	_____
4.	_____	4.	_____	4.	_____
5.	_____	5.	_____	5.	_____

	dull		hide		start
1.	_____	1.	_____	1.	_____
2.	_____	2.	_____	2.	_____
3.	_____	3.	_____	3.	_____
4.	_____	4.	_____	4.	_____
5.	_____	5.	_____	5.	_____

COLOR IT YOUR WAY

Read this story.

Then use a dictionary to find a more colorful word for each underlined word.

Rewrite the story with the more colorful words.

Add a last line to make the story more interesting.

The sea was crystal clear and very <u>peaceful</u>. Seagulls were <u>flying</u> through the sky, <u>looking</u> for some tasty fish. The sand was <u>soft</u>, and shells were <u>plentiful</u>. It was a <u>glorious</u> morning to be alive.

_____

_____

_____

_____

_____

_____

_____

_____

_____

_____

_____

_____

IN THE MOONLIGHT

Read the groups of words.

If the words form a sentence, place the correct punctuation mark at the end.

If the group of words forms a phrase, go on to the next group.

Color the spaces in the puzzle that show the numbers of the *sentences*.

Do *not* color the spaces that show the numbers of phrases.

Hint: Use your blue crayon to color the picture.

1. The moon gives light at night
2. A full moon
3. The moon moves around the earth
4. One bright night
5. The moon's trip around the earth takes 4 weeks
6. Have you ever seen a full moon
7. In the shining moonlight

A LAMB'S TALE

Read the story below.
Then supply the correct punctuation and write
3 sentences to complete the story.

Once upon a time long long ago a wooly white
lamb was owned by a little girl named Mary The
lamb had a very bad habit of following Mary to
school each day To tell the truth Mary liked having
the lamb at school   but the teacher had a different
opinion

Oh no not again   the teacher would say   Mary
why did you bring that lamb to school

Please teacher Mary would say _____

_____

_____

_____

_____

_____

_____

_____

_____

_____

_____

_____

SPELLING BEE

Good writers need to be good spellers.
Fill this spelling bee's wings with words you can spell.

MY FAVORITE ANIMAL

1. Write a declarative sentence to tell about your favorite animal.

   _____

   _____

2. Write an interrogative sentence to ask a friend what his or her favorite animal is.

   _____

   _____

3. Write an imperative sentence giving a command to an animal.

   _____

   _____

4. Write an exclamatory sentence praising the animal for obeying your command.

   _____

   _____

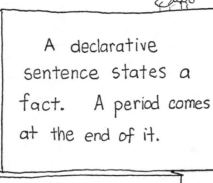

A declarative sentence states a fact. A period comes at the end of it.

An imperative sentence gives a command, and a period comes at the end of it, too.

An interrogative sentence asks a question and has a question mark at the end of it.

An exclamatory sentence expresses strong feeling or emotion, and an exclamation point comes at the end of it.

HOW'S THE WEATHER?

Write one complete sentence to give a weather report for each scene below.

_____

_____

_____

_____

_____

_____

_____

_____

SIGNS AND SENTENCES

Write a complete sentence to tell what each of these signs means.

1. _____

_____

2. _____

_____

3. _____

_____

4. _____

_____

EARTHLY DELIGHTS

Separate each of the following run-on sentences to make 2 complete sentences.
Place a period at the end of each sentence.
Capitalize the first word of the second sentence.

1. Earthworms are content in the earth it is dark and damp

    _____

    _____

2. They do not like sunlight they do not like dryness

    _____

    _____

3. Earthworms dig their burrows by eating the earth they digest it as they crawl

    _____

    _____

4. Their burrows bring air to the roots of plants this aids the plants' growth

    _____

    _____

5. Common enemies of the earthworm are the robin and mole the centipede and platypus are enemies too

    _____

    _____

FOUR BIRTHDAYS A YEAR

Birthdays are a lot of fun, but unfortunately they come only once a year on Earth. That's because it takes Earth 365 days to make one revolution around the sun. If you could fly to the planet Mercury, though, you could have 4 birthdays in a year because it takes only 88 Earth days for Mercury to revolve around the sun.

If you could have 4 birthdays a year . . .

1. Write a sentence to tell how you would spend your winter birthday.

_____

_____

2. Write a sentence to tell how you would spend your spring birthday.

_____

_____

3. Write a sentence to tell how you would spend your summer birthday.

_____

_____

4. Write a sentence to tell how you would spend your fall birthday.

_____

_____

THE BIG DISCOVERY

Write a complete sentence to tell what you would do in each of the following situations.

1. You find an elephant on your back porch. _____
_____
_____

2. After you give him some food, he sits down in your mother's lounge chair. _____
_____
_____

3. He falls asleep and begins to snore very loudly.
_____
_____

4. The neighbor's dog runs over barking.

WHOSE SCHOOL?

Brandon thinks students have more fun than teachers. He says that teachers have to come to school earlier and stay later than kids.

Marilou thinks teachers make all the rules and have more freedom to do as they choose. She says that teachers come to school because they want to and kids come because they have to.

Do you agree with Brandon or with Marilou?

Write a paragraph telling what you think.

Check your work for correct spelling and punctuation.

CHANGE OVER

Think of something you would like to change about your life.

Then write a paragraph to tell how you could begin to make that change.

SELECT YOUR TOPIC

Select one of the topics below and write a paragraph about it.

Remember to indent and check your work for correct punctuation.

What I Like About my Teacher
The Best Trip I've Ever Taken
A Pet I Would Like To Own

_____

_____

_____

_____

_____

_____

_____

_____

_____

DAILY FARE

Twice a day, pandas at the National Zoo in Washington, D.C., are fed the following diet:

MENU:
carrots
apples
sweet potatoes
rice mixed with milk
bamboo
dog biscuits
vitamins
honey sandwiches

Write a paragraph to tell about feeding time for the pandas.

_____

_____

_____

_____

_____

_____

_____

_____

_____

_____

FLYING HIGH

Look at this picture carefully.
Write a paragraph to tell what will happen next.

_____

_____

_____

_____

_____

_____

_____

_____

A LUCKY ENDING

Number the sentences below to show the natural order in which they occurred.

Then rewrite the sentences in paragraph form on the lines below.

Don't forget to indent and use correct punctuation and spelling.

____ The spectators watched in wonder to see what would happen next.

____ Then, all of a sudden, one of the engines stopped.

____ The plane hovered for a few seconds and then started dropping quickly.

____ The plane taxied down the runway and slowly went up into the sky.

____ They were relieved to see the pilot and copilot parachute to the ground safely.

_____

_____

_____

_____

_____

_____

_____

_____

_____

_____

_____

COMPOSITION
AND
ORIGINAL
WRITING

THE BIG GAME

Read the paragraph below.
Then design a poster to advertise the game.
Be sure that the poster includes the **who, what, when,** and **where.**

The Fast Runners softball team will play the Great Hitters team at two o'clock in the afternoon on Monday, June 29. Tickets will cost $1.00 for adults and $ .50 for children under 12. The game will take place at City Road Park on 79th Street.

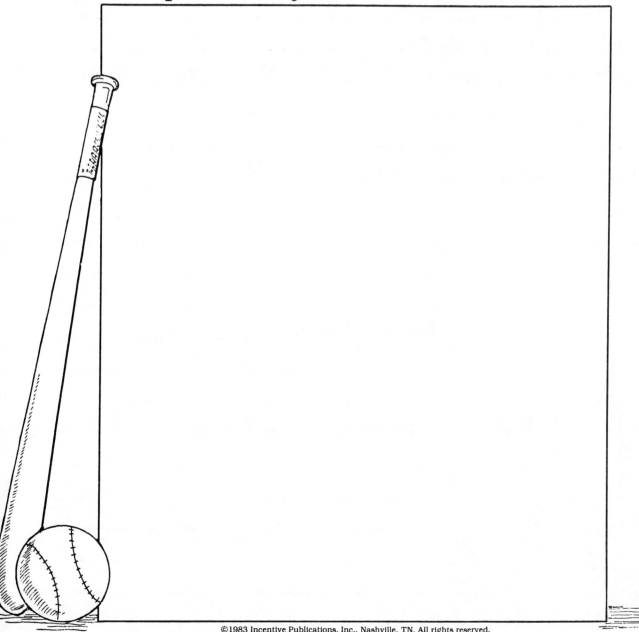

BIOGRAPHICAL INTERVIEW

Interview a classmate you find interesting.

Fill out this biographical data sheet and use the information to write the person's biography.

Remember, a biography must include *facts*, not fiction.

Name _____

Parents' Names _____

Date of Birth _____

Place of Birth _____

Weight and Length at Birth _____

Favorite Things (sport, toy, song, TV program, foods)

_____

_____

Names and Ages of Brothers and/or Sisters _____

_____

_____

Special Talents _____

_____

Three Wishes _____

_____

_____

Other Important Facts

_____

_____

_____

_____

AN INTERESTING LIFE STORY

Use the information gathered on the biographical data sheet to write a biography.

A *biography* must be a true account of the person's life. The writer can add interest by including the most exciting events and by using colorful and creative words and sentences.

This is a biography of _____

_____

_____

_____

_____

_____

_____

_____

_____

_____

_____

_____

_____

_____

_____

_____

_____

THE PERFECT BIRTHDAY GIFT

Have you ever wrapped a birthday gift?

It is a step-by-step task.

Here are the steps for wrapping a gift.

The steps are mixed up.

Read all the steps first.

Then place the steps in correct order by numbering them 1-9.

___Tie a bow at the top of the gift.

___Cut the amount of paper you will need.

___Gather together the gift box, tape, wrapping paper, scissors, and ribbon or yarn.

___The gift is ready to give!

___Place the box on the wrapping paper. Estimate how much paper you will need.

___Fold the paper together at each side. Place a piece of tape on each side.

___Pull ribbon or yarn around the box. Allow extra ribbon for a bow. Cut as much ribbon as you think you will need.

___Place the gift box face-down on the wrapping paper. Pull the paper together at the top. Place a piece of tape there.

___Turn the wrapped gift so the box is face-up. The seam of the wrapping paper will be at the bottom.

JUST SUPPOSE

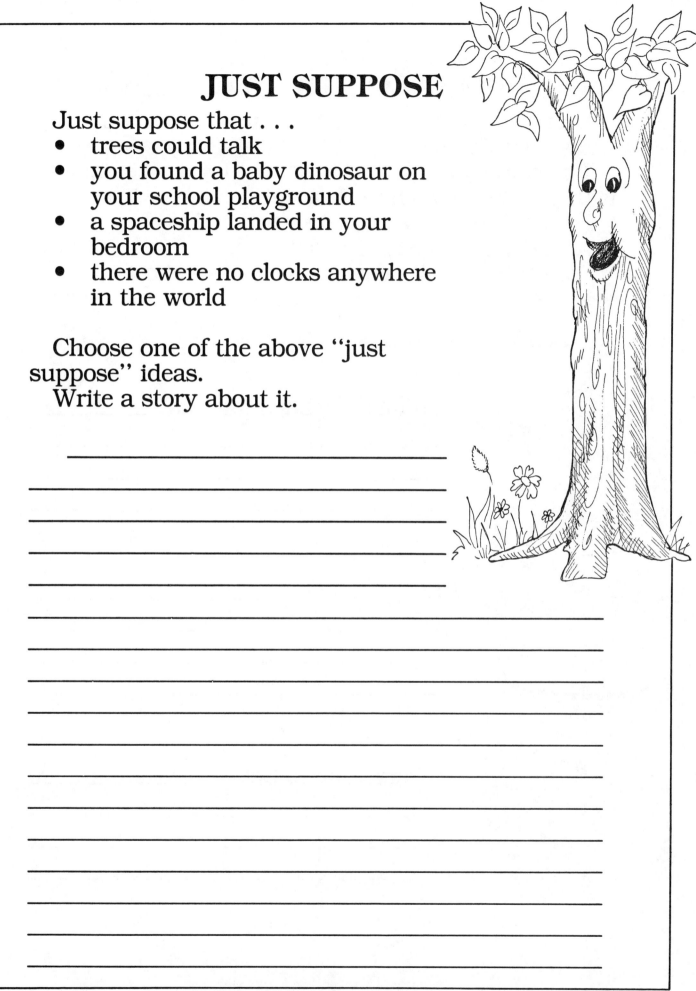

Just suppose that . . .
- trees could talk
- you found a baby dinosaur on your school playground
- a spaceship landed in your bedroom
- there were no clocks anywhere in the world

Choose one of the above "just suppose" ideas.
Write a story about it.

A CATALOG OF CLOTHES

Many people order clothes by mail instead of shopping in stores.

The companies that sell the clothes mail catalogs with pictures and short descriptions of the items.

People look at the pictures and read the descriptions, then decide what to buy.

For each catalog item below, write a short description that will make a person want to order it.

Genuine Alaskan Mukluks _____

_____

_____

_____

Brainy Beany _____

_____

_____

_____

Personalized Belt _____

_____

_____

_____

CONSONANT CHARACTERS

Write a silly consonant story to fit each of the characters below. In each story, use as many words as possible that begin with the same letter as the character's name.

Billy Bubbles

Billy Bubbles blows better bubbles than Betty Berry or Bart Brown. He brings bread and butter for breakfast and beef and beans for lunch.

Sad Sam _____

_____

_____

_____

_____

_____

Playful Patty _____

_____

_____

_____

_____

_____

QUESTION TIME

You are usually asked to write answers to questions.

This time, you write the questions.

1. Question: _____
   Answer: A big fat hen.

2. Question: _____
   Answer: Money.

3. Question: _____
   Answer: A rocking rabbit.

4. Question: _____
   Answer: Mealtime magic.

5. Question: _____
   Answer: Over the rainbow.

6. Question: _____
   Answer: A hungry cowboy.

THE TALE OF THE TAIL

Dogs, of course, wag their tails when they are pleased. But did you know that when the tail twitches only at the end, your dog may be bored or irritated? The lower a dog holds its tail, the less confidence it has. If your dog curls its tail between its legs, it probably feels afraid or defeated. A tail that is held straight out behind indicates a lively, alert animal.

How do you show your emotions?

Write a complete sentence to tell how you act when:

You are happy. _____

_____

You are sad. _____

_____

You are afraid. _____

_____

You are surprised. _____

_____

A VISIT FROM OUTER SPACE

Use your pencil to finish the spaceship below.
Then use your imagination to complete the
information sheet.

Name of spaceship _____

Description _____

_____

_____

Planet your spaceship is from

_____

Description of planet _____

_____

_____

_____

A SILLY STORY

Fill each of the critters below with descriptive words.

Then select one of the critters and write a silly story about it. Use *all* your descriptive words in the story.

Give your story the best possible title to tell a reader what the story is about.

_____

_____

_____

_____

_____

_____

_____

_____

_____

_____

_____

RIDDLE ZOO

Read and solve the animal riddles.
Then write a 4-line riddle for one other
animal from the Riddle Zoo.

Maybe I live in the jungle
Or in a circus or a zoo,
But I carry my own trunk
Wherever I go.

I am an _____

I have spots all over
And long, skinny legs
A pain in my neck
Is a long, long pain.

I am a _____

ANIMAL ADVENTURE

Cut **2** pictures of animals from a magazine. Cut the animals apart and glue together parts from the **2** to make a funny animal.

Name the animal and write a creative story about an adventure the animal might have.

_____

_____

_____

_____

_____

_____

_____

_____

_____

_____

_____

_____

_____

_____

_____

WRITE A LETTER

Select one of the following letters.
Write it in the space below.

____ Cinderella's letter to her stepmother, written a
week after her marriage to the prince

____ Goldilocks's letter to Baby Bear, apologizing for
breaking his chair

____ Snow White's farewell letter to the dwarves

Dear _____,

_____

_____

_____

_____

_____

_____

_____

_____

_____

Yours truly,

_____

A BETTER LETTER

Write a letter to a boy or girl in another country.

Tell the person about your school, your teacher, and your friends.

Remember . . .

The *heading* gives your address and the date.
The *greeting* tells who will receive the letter.
The *body* carries your message.
The *closing* is a sign-off from you.
The *signature* gives your name.

TELL IT LIKE IT IS

An *autobiography* is the story of one person's life, written by that person.

An autobiography includes facts about time and place of birth, family, schools attended, and places lived. A good autobiography also includes things of interest such as hobbies, friends, funny incidents, likes, dislikes, and dreams for the future.

Write your autobiography here.

_____

_____

_____

_____

_____

_____

_____

_____

_____

_____

_____

_____

PRODUCT PROGRESS

Look around your room and find 2 products that were not in use 10 years ago. Write the names of the objects.

1. _____

2. _____

Now think of 2 products that could be designed for use during the next 10 years. Try to be as creative as possible and think of products that would be exciting as well as useful. Name your products and write a short description of each.

1. _____
(name)

_____

_____

_____

2. _____
(name)

_____

_____

_____

_____

THREE INTERESTING CHARACTERS

Look carefully at each person pictured below.
Give each person a name.
Write 3 characteristics which describe each person.
Write what you think each person's hobby might be.

_____
(name)

_____
_____
_____
_____

_____
(name)

_____
_____
_____
_____

_____
(name)

_____
_____
_____
_____

READY FOR TAKEOFF

Place your fist in the box below and trace around it with your pencil.

Add features to the traced shape to make it into a spacecraft to travel to another planet.

Then fill out the information for the spacecraft.

Spacecraft Information

Name _____

Description _____

_____

_____

Planet to be visited _____

On a separate sheet of paper, write the story of the trip.

COLOR AND WRITE

Try to use every crayon you have to color this picture.

Write 1 sentence to describe the butterfly.

Write 1 sentence to describe the flowers.

Write 1 sentence to describe the trees.

_____

_____

_____

_____

_____

EXPLAIN IT

Look in a magazine for a picture of an unusual
animal or an animal in an unusual setting.
Cut it out and glue it in the square below.

GLUE

Write 10 words that describe the animal. On
another sheet of paper use the words in a paragraph
to explain to someone *exactly* how the animal looks.

_____   _____

_____   _____

_____   _____

_____   _____

_____   _____

LOOK INTO THE CRYSTAL BALL

This picture appeared in the wizard's crystal ball.

Use your crayons to color and add whatever you wish to the picture to make it more exciting.

Look at the new picture you have created. Write the story it tells here.

_____

_____

_____

_____

_____

_____

COOKIE JAR

Write the conversation that is taking place.
Then draw a panel to show what will happen next.

FINGER TALK

Finish each finger puppet below.

Write a puppet play for the characters you have created.

Then cut out the puppets and present your play.

_____

_____

_____

_____

_____

_____

_____

_____

_____

_____

ELEPHANTS DON'T MAKE GOOD PETS

Write the conversation that is taking place.

THE ROCKING CHAIR MYSTERY

Who is this gentleman?
Where did he come from?
Why is he sitting here?
Write his life story.

WRITE THE STORY

Select one of these titles for the picture:
- ☐ An Upside-Down Day
- ☐ A Funny Forest
- ☐ An Animal Mix-Up

Write a story to go with it.

_____

_____

_____

_____

_____

_____

_____

_____

A GOOD LUCK STORY

Write a sentence to tell what you think about when you see a picture of a four-leaf clover.

_____

Then finish the story below.

Good Luck for Mandy

Mandy dried her tears and smiled. Then she picked the four-leaf clover. _____

_____

_____

_____

_____

_____

_____

_____

_____

_____

_____

_____

_____

_____

POET AT WORK

<u>P</u>ick up your pencil and
<u>O</u>pen your mind.
<u>E</u>ach boy and girl can
<u>M</u>ake poems that rhyme.

   This fun poetry is called an
acrostic. The word that the
poem tells about is written
vertically down the left-hand side
of the paper, and each line
across begins with one of the
word's letters.

   Write an acrostic in the box below.

RHYME TIME

Draw lines to connect the rhyming words.
Then use the words to write rhyming couplets.

goat   frown
can   bed
cat   pan
red   coat
brown   hat

1. The funny old <u>goat</u>
   Is wearing a new <u>coat</u>.

2. _____

   _____

3. _____

   _____

4. _____

   _____

5. _____

   _____